KING RICHARD III

Books should be returned or renewed by the
last date stamped above

**KENT
ARTS &
LIBRARIES**

**Kent
County
Council**
ARTS & LIBRARIES

Shakespeare The Animated Tales is a multinational venture conceived by S4C,
Channel 4 Wales. Produced in Russia, Wales and England, the series has been financed by S4C
and the BBC (UK), Christmas Films (Russia), Home Box Office (USA) and Fujisankei (Japan).

Academic Panel
Professor Stanley Wells
Dr Rex Gibson

Educational Adviser
Michael Marland

Publishing Editor and Co-ordinator
Jane Fior

Book Design
Fiona Macmillan and Ness Wood

Animation Director for *King Richard III*
Natalia Orlova of Christmas Films, Moscow

Series Editors
Martin Lamb and Penelope Middelboe, Right Angle, Tenby, Wales

Executive Producers
Christopher Grace (S4C)
Elizabeth Babakhina (Christmas Films)

Associate Producer
Theresa Plummer Andrews (BBC)

First published in 1994
by William Heinemann Ltd
an imprint of Reed Consumer Books Ltd
Michelin House, 81 Fulham Road, London SW3 6RB
and Auckland, Melbourne, Singapore and Toronto
Copyright © Shakespeare Animated Films/Christmas Films 1994

ISBN 0 434 96783 1

A CIP catalogue record for this title is available
from the British Library

Printed and bound in the UK by BPC Paulton Books Limited

The publishers would like to thank Paul Cox
for the series logo illustration,
Carol Kemp for her calligraphy,
Theo Crosby for the use of his painting of the Globe,
and Rosa Fior and Celia Salisbury Jones
for their help on the books.

Shakespeare
THE ANIMATED TALES

KING RICHARD III

ABRIDGED BY LEON GARFIELD

ILLUSTRATED BY PETER KOTOV

HEINEMANN YOUNG BOOKS

Martin Droeshout sculpsit London.

WILLIAM SHAKESPEARE

NEXT TO GOD, A wise man once said, Shakespeare created most. In the thirty-seven plays that are his chief legacy to the world – and surely no-one ever left a richer! – human nature is displayed in all its astonishing variety.

He has enriched the stage with matchless comedies, tragedies, histories, and, towards the end of his life, with plays that defy all description, strange plays that haunt the imagination like visions.

His range is enormous: kings and queens, priests, princes and merchants, soldiers, clowns and drunkards, murderers, pimps, whores, fairies, monsters and pale, avenging ghosts 'strut and fret their hour upon the stage'. Murders and suicides abound; swords flash, blood flows, poison drips, and lovers sigh; yet there is always time for old men to talk of growing apples and for gardeners to discuss the weather.

In the four hundred years since they were written, they have become known and loved in every land; they are no longer the property of one country and one people, they are the priceless possession of the world.

His life, from what we know of it, was not astonishing. The stories that have attached themselves to him are remarkable only for their ordinariness: poaching deer, sleeping off a drinking bout under a wayside tree. There are no duels, no loud, passionate loves, no excesses of any kind. He was not one of your unruly geniuses whose habits are more interesting than their works. From all accounts, he was of a gentle, honourable disposition, a good businessman, and a careful father.

He was born on April 23rd 1564, to John and Mary Shakespeare of Henley Street, Stratford-upon-Avon. He was their third child and first son. When he was four or five he began his education at the local petty school. He left the local grammar school when he was about fourteen, in all probability to help in his father's glove-making shop. When he was eighteen, he married Anne Hathaway, who lived in a nearby village. By the time he was twenty-one, he was the father of three children, two daughters and a son.

Then, it seems, a restless mood came upon him. Maybe he travelled, maybe he was, as some say, a schoolmaster in the country; but at some time during the next seven years, he went to London and found employment in the theatre. When he was twenty-eight, he was already well enough known as an actor and playwright to excite the spiteful envy of a rival, who referred to him as 'an upstart crow'.

He mostly lived and worked in London until his mid-forties, when he returned to his family and home in Stratford, where he remained in prosperous circumstances until his death on April 23rd 1616, his fifty-second birthday.

He left behind him a widow, two daughters (his son died in childhood), and the richest imaginary world ever created by the human mind.

LEON GARFIELD

The list of the plays contained in the First Folio of 1623. This was the first collected edition of Shakespeare's plays and was gathered together by two of his fellow actors, John Hemmings and Henry Condell.

A CATALOGVE

of the seuerall Comedies, Histories, and Tragedies contained in this Volume.

The Theatre in Shakespeare's Day

IN 1989 AN ARCHAEOLOGICAL discovery was made on the south bank of the Thames that sent shivers of delight through the theatre world. A fragment of Shakespeare's own theatre, the Globe, where many of his plays were first performed, had been found.

This discovery has fuelled further interest in how Shakespeare himself conceived and staged his plays. We know a good deal already, and archaeology as well as documentary research will no doubt reveal more, but although we can only speculate on some of the details, we have a good idea of what the Elizabethan theatre-goer saw, heard and smelt when he went to see a play by William Shakespeare at the Globe.

It was an entirely different experience from anything we know today. Modern theatres have roofs to keep out the weather. If it rained on the Globe, forty per cent of the play-goers got wet. Audiences today sit on cushioned seats, and usually (especially if the play is by Shakespeare) watch and listen in respectful silence. In the Globe, the floor of the theatre was packed with a riotous crowd of garlic-reeking apprentices, house servants and artisans, who had each paid a penny to stand for the entire duration of the play, to buy nuts and apples from the food-sellers, to refresh themselves with bottled ale, relieve themselves, perhaps, into buckets by the back wall, to talk, cheer, catcall, clap and hiss if the play did not please them.

In the galleries that rose in curved tiers around the inside of the building sat those who could afford to pay two pennies for a seat, and the benefits of a roof over their heads. Here, the middle ranking citizens, the merchants, the sea captains, the clerks from the Inns of Court, would sit crammed into their small eighteen inch space and look down upon the 'groundlings' below. In the 'Lords' room', the rich and the great, noblemen and women, courtiers and foreign ambassadors had to pay sixpence each for the relative comfort and luxury of their exclusive position directly above the stage, where they smoked tobacco, and overlooked the rest.

We are used to a stage behind an arch, with wings on either side, from which the actors come on and into which they disappear. In the Globe, the stage was a platform thrusting out into the middle of the floor, and the audience, standing in the central yard, surrounded it on three sides. There were no wings. Three doors at the back of the stage were used for all exits and entrances. These were sometimes covered by a curtain, which could be used as a prop.

Today we sit in a darkened theatre or cinema, and look at a brilliantly lit stage or screen, or we sit at home in a small, private world of our own, watching a luminous television screen. The close-packed, rowdy crowd at the Globe, where the play started at two o'clock in the afternoon, had no artificial light to enhance their illusion. It was the words that moved them. They came to listen, rather than to see.

No dimming lights announced the start of the play. A blast from a trumpet and three sharp knocks warned the audience that the action was about to begin. In the broad daylight, the actor could see the audience as clearly as the audience could see him. He spoke directly to the crowd, and held them with his eyes, following their reactions. He could play up to the raucous laughter that greeted the comical, bawdy scenes, and gauge the emotional response to the higher flights of poetry. Sometimes he even improvised speeches of his own. He was surrounded by, enfolded by, his audience.

The stage itself would seem uncompromisingly bare to our eyes. There was no scenery. No painted backdrops suggested a forest, or a castle, or the sumptuous interior of a palace. Shakespeare painted the scenery with his words, and the imagination of the audience did the rest.

Props were brought onto the stage only when they were essential for the action. A bed would be carried on when a character needed to lie on it. A throne would be let down from above when a king needed to sit on it. Torches and lanterns would suggest that it was dark, but the main burden of persuading an audience, at three o'clock in the afternoon, that it was in fact the middle of the night, fell upon the language.

In our day, costume designers create a concept as part of the production of a play into which each costume fits. Shakespeare's actors were responsible for their own costumes. They would use what was to hand in the 'tiring house' (dressing room), or supplement it out of their own pockets. Classical, medieval and Tudor clothes could easily appear side by side in the same play.

No women actors appeared on a public stage until many years after

The Workes of William Shakespeare,

containing all his Comedies, Histories, and
Tragedies : Truely set forth, according to their first
ORIGINALL.

The Names of the Principall Actors
in all these Playes.

William Shakespeare.	Samuel Gilburne.
Richard Burbadge.	Robert Armin.
John Hemmings.	William Ostler.
Augustine Phillips.	Nathan Field.
William Kempt.	John Underwood.
Thomas Poope.	Nicholas Tooley.
George Bryan.	William Ecclestone.
Henry Condell.	Joseph Taylor.
William Slye.	Robert Benfield.
Richard Cowly.	Robert Goughe.
John Lowine.	Richard Robinson.
Samuell Crosse.	Iohn Shancke.
Alexander Cooke.	Iohn Rice.

Shakespeare's death, for at that time it would have been considered shameless. The parts of young girls were played by boys. The parts of older women were played by older men.

In 1613 the Globe theatre was set on fire by a spark from a cannon during a performance of Henry VIII, and it burnt to the ground. The actors, including Shakespeare himself, dug into their own pockets and paid for it to be rebuilt. The new theatre lasted until 1642, when it closed again. Now, in the 1990s, the Globe is set to rise again as a committed band of actors, scholars and enthusiasts are raising the money to rebuild Shakespeare's theatre in its original form a few yards from its previous site.

From the time when the first Globe theatre was built until today, Shakespeare's plays have been performed in a vast variety of languages, styles, costumes and techniques, on stage, on film, on television and in animated film. Shakespeare himself, working within the round wooden walls of his theatre, would have been astonished by it all.

PATRICK SPOTTISWOODE
Director of Education,
Globe Theatre Museum

From this list of actors, we can see that William Shakespeare not only wrote plays but also acted in them. The Globe theatre, where these actors performed, is now being rebuilt close to its original site on the south bank of the river Thames.

SHAKESPEARE TODAY

SHAKESPEARE IS ALIVE TODAY! Although William Shakespeare the man lies long buried in Stratford-upon-Avon parish church, he lives on in countless millions of hearts and minds.

Imagine that cold April day in 1616. The small funeral procession labours slowly along Church Street. Huge black horses draw the wooden cart bearing the simple coffin. On the coffin, a few daffodils and primroses, plucked only minutes before from the garden of New Place, gravely nod with each jolt and jar of the rutted road.

Most of Stratford's citizens have turned out, muffled against the biting wind, to see the last appearance of their wealthy neighbour. You couldn't call it a crowd. Just small respectful groups clustering the dry places on the roadside, careful to avoid the mud splashed up by the great hooves of the lumbering horses.

Men and women briefly bow their heads as the dead man and the black-clad mourners pass. The townspeople share their opinions, as neighbours do. "He used to do some acting, didn't he?" "Made a lot of money in London. Writing plays, I think." "Used to come home once a year to see his family, but nobody here really knew a lot about Master Shakespeare." "Wasn't he a poet?" "Big landowner hereabouts anyway. All those fields over at Welcombe."

Past the Guild Chapel where he had worshipped as a boy. Past the school where long ago his imagination was fired by language. At the churchyard gate, under the sad elms, six men effortlessly heave the coffin on to their shoulders. William Shakespeare is about to enter his parish church for the last time.

Nobody at that long ago funeral guessed that they were saying goodbye to a man who would become the most famous Englishman of his age – perhaps of all time.

Shakespeare lives on. He weaves familiar themes into his tales: the conflicts between parents and children, love at first sight, the power struggles of war and politics. His language is heard everywhere. If you ever call someone 'a blinking idiot' or 'a tower of strength', or describe them as 'tongue-tied', or suffering from 'green-eyed jealousy', or being 'dead as a doornail', you are speaking the language of Shakespeare.

If you say 'it was Greek to me' or 'parting is such sweet sorrow', or that something is 'too much of a good thing' and that you 'have not slept one wink', the words of Shakespeare are alive in your mouth. Shakespeare's language has a power all of its own, rich in emotional intensity. Because he was a poet who wrote plays, he could make even the simplest words utterly memorable. All around the world people know Hamlet's line 'To be or not to be, that is the question.'

Shakespeare is still performed today because of the electrifying power of his storytelling. Whether his story is about love or murder, or kings and queens, he keeps you on the edge of your seat wanting to know what happens next.

He created well over nine hundred characters in his plays. However large or small the part, each character springs vividly to life in performance. They live in our imagination because they are so much like people today. They experience the same emotions that everyone feels and recognises: love, jealousy, fear, courage, ambition, pride … and a hundred others.

In every play, Shakespeare invites us to imagine what the characters are like, and for nearly four hundred years people have accepted Shakespeare's invitation. The plays have been re-imagined in very many ways. They have been shortened, added to, and set in very different periods of history. They have been translated into many languages and performed all over the world. Shakespeare lives because all persons in every age and every society can make their own interpretations and performances of Shakespeare.

The creators of *The Animated Tales* have re-imagined *King Richard III* in a 26 minute animated film. You too can make your own living Shakespeare. Read the text that follows, and watch the video. Then try reading the play either by yourself, changing your voice to suit the different characters, or with friends, and record it on a tape recorder. If you have a toy theatre, try staging it with characters and scenery that you make and paint yourself. Or collect together a cast and create your own production for your family and friends.

Dr Rex Gibson

Dr Rex Gibson is the director of the Shakespeare and Schools Project which is part of the Institute of Education at the University of Cambridge.

In 1994 he was awarded the Sam Wanamaker International Shakespeare Award for his outstanding contribution to the world's knowledge of the works of Shakespeare.

What They Said of Him

One will ever find, in searching his works, new cause for astonishment and admiration.

Goethe

Shakespeare was a writer of all others the most calculated to make his readers better as well as wiser.

Samuel Taylor Coleridge

An overstrained enthusiasm is more pardonable with respect to Shakespeare than the want of it; for our admiration cannot easily surpass his genius.

William Hazlitt

It required three hundred years for England to begin to hear those two words that the whole world cries in her ear – William Shakespeare.

Victor Hugo

He has left nothing to be said about nothing or anything.

John Keats

The stream of time, which is continually washing the dissoluble fabrics of other poets, passes without injury by the adamant of Shakespeare.

Samuel Johnson

KING RICHARD III

The Tragedy of King Richard III is the story of a royal monster, a misshapen devil by name of Richard, Duke of Gloucester. At the very beginning of the play, Shakespeare seems to hurl him onto the stage so that he limps and stumbles out of the shadows, almost unwillingly into the light. "I am determined to prove a villain," he confides; and does so with a vengeance as he claws his bloody way to the throne, murdering all who stand in his path, even little children: "I fear no uncles dead," says one of his nephews. "Nor none that live, I hope," protests his murderous uncle, and sends the child and his little brother to their deaths in the grim Tower of London. At length, even his own mother is driven to curse him: "Bloody thou art, bloody will be thy end!" And so it is.

THE CHARACTERS IN THE PLAY

in order of appearance

RICHARD	*Duke of Gloucester, later King Richard III*
THE DUKE OF CLARENCE	*his brother*
LADY ANNE	*widow of Edward, Prince of Wales*
TWO MURDERERS	
THE DUKE OF BUCKINGHAM	
QUEEN ELIZABETH	*wife to King Edward IV*
EDWARD	*Prince of Wales, her son*
THE DUKE OF YORK	*her younger son*
THE ARCHBISHOP OF YORK	
LORD HASTINGS	*the Lord Chamberlain*
LORD CARDINAL BOURCHIER	*The Archbishop of Canterbury*
SIR WILLIAM CATESBY	
THE BISHOP OF ELY	
THE DUCHESS OF YORK	*mother of Richard, Edward IV and the Duke of Clarence*
SIR JAMES TYRREL	
MESSENGER	
THE DUKE OF NORFOLK	
THE EARL OF RICHMOND	*afterwards King Henry VII*
	Lords, soldiers, servants and attendants

The curtain rises on the Palace of Westminster, dark against a bloodshot sky. A black misshapen figure crawls up onto the battlements and, like a malevolent spider, crouches over the town below.

RICHARD   Now is the winter of our discontent made glorious summer by this son of York.

The winter of discontent is the long civil war between the houses of York and Lancaster. The glorious son of York is the victor King Edward IV, and the speaker is his brother Richard Duke of Gloucester.

RICHARD   But I that am deform'd, unfinish'd, have no delight to pass away the time, and therefore, since I cannot prove a lover, I am determined to prove a villain . . .

King Edward is sick; and so is the kingdom. Fear, greed, treachery and hatred set family against family, mother against son, and brother against brother. A fierce ambition burns in the dark heart of the king's hunchback brother: he will be king! Already he has murdered Henry VI and his son, Edward, but others of his own family still stand in his way, even his brother George, Duke of Clarence.

Along a stony passageway comes the Duke of Clarence, between armed guards. Suddenly the figure of Richard emerges from the darkness and stands in the way.

RICHARD   Brother, good day; what means this armed guard?

CLARENCE   His majesty hath appointed this conduct to convey me to the Tower.

RICHARD   Upon what cause?

CLARENCE   Because my name is George. A wizard told him that by 'G' his issue disinherited should be. And for my name of George begins with 'G', it follows in his thought that I am he.

RICHARD   Brother, farewell. I will unto the king. Your imprisonment shall not be long; I will deliver you, or else lie for you.

Clarence is marched away by the guard. Richard, smiling, stares after them. He rubs his hands with complicity.

RICHARD   Go, tread the path that thou shalt ne'er return; I do love thee so that I will shortly send thy soul to Heaven –

Richard is in his apartment, preening himself before a mirror. He puts on his rings, admiring the glitter of the precious stones. He is one step nearer. But he needs to be respectable, he needs a well-born wife, and who better than the Lady Anne?

A noise outside attracts Richard's attention. He sees from his window Lady Anne in mourning and gentlemen with halberds, following a coffin. The procession stops in front of his windows.

RICHARD   (*stepping back from the window*) I'll marry Warwick's youngest daughter. What though I kill'd her husband and her father?

ANNE   (*gazing at the coffin.*) Poor key-cold figure of a holy king . . . be it lawful that I invoke thy ghost to hear the lamentations of poor Anne.

Suddenly a huge shadow falls over her. Anne turns around. Richard appears in front of the procession.

RICHARD   Villains, set down the corse!

The bearers lower the coffin and retreat in fear.

ANNE   Foul devil, for God's sake hence, and trouble us not.

RICHARD   Sweet saint, for charity, be not so curst.

ANNE   (*to bearers*) O gentlemen! see, see dead Henry's wounds open their congeal'd mouths and bleed afresh! Blush, blush thou lump of foul deformity, for 'tis thy presence that exhales this blood!

RICHARD   Lady, you know no rules of charity –

ANNE   Villain, thou know'st no law of God nor man! Didst thou not kill this king?

RICHARD   (*coming closer to Anne and speaking softly*) I grant ye. The better for the King of Heaven, that hath him.

ANNE   And thou unfit for any place but hell.

RICHARD   (*going around Anne*) Yes, one place else.

ANNE   Some dungeon?

RICHARD   (*stopping in front of Anne*) Your bed-chamber.

ANNE   (*spitting at him*) Out of my sight!

RICHARD   Your beauty was the cause, your beauty, that did haunt me in my sleep to undertake the death of all the world.

ANNE   (*covering her face with her hands*) If I thought that, I tell thee, homicide, these nails should rend that beauty from my cheeks.

RICHARD   Teach not thy lip such scorn; for it was made for kissing, lady, not for such contempt. If thy revengeful heart cannot forgive, lo, here I lend thee this sharp-pointed sword.

He kneels and, offering his sword, bares his breast. She takes the sword but, trembling, cannot strike the blow.

RICHARD   Nay, do not pause; for I did kill King Henry, but 'twas thy beauty that provoked me. Nay, now dispatch; 'twas I that stabb'd young Edward, but 'twas thy heavenly face that set me on. Take up the sword again, or take up me.

ANNE   I would I knew thy heart.

RICHARD   Vouchsafe to wear this ring.

Richard takes Anne's hand and puts a ring on her finger.

ANNE   To take is not to give.

RICHARD   Look how my ring encompasseth thy finger; even so thy breast encloseth my poor heart.

The procession departs, leaving Richard alone. He hops along, well pleased with himself, and his long misshapen shadow accompanies him.

RICHARD   (*to shadow*) Was ever woman in this humour woo'd? Was ever woman in this humour won? I'll have her, but I will not keep her long.

In the semi-darkness of King Edward's bedchamber the queen and relatives stand about his bed. Richard looks in and sees the queen make a few steps and kneel in front of a crucifix. The king's sickness has deepened and the queen is full of dread. Should he die, her sons are too young to rule. With George, Duke of Clarence, in the Tower, Richard, the third brother, will be Protector. And the venomous hunchback hates her and her family.

RICHARD   He cannot live, I hope, and must not die till George be pack'd with post-horse up to Heaven.

In a small, gloomy room in the Tower, lit by moonlight coming through the narrow windows, the Duke of Clarence lies upon his bed. His sleep is uneasy. Shadows fall across his face. He wakes. Two murderers stare down on him.

CLARENCE   In God's name, what art thou?

1ST MURDERER   A man, as you are.

CLARENCE   Who sent you hither? Wherefore do you come?

2ND MURDERER   To –

CLARENCE   To murder me? (*They nod.*) Wherein, my friends have I offended you?

1ST MURDERER   Offended us you have not, but the king; therefore prepare to die.

CLARENCE   I will send you to my brother Gloucester who shall reward you better for my life than Edward will for tidings of my death.

2ND MURDERER   You are deceiv'd: your brother Gloucester hates you.

1ST MURDERER   'Tis he that sends us to destroy you here.

He struggles from his bed and holds out his hands, pleadingly, to second murderer. The first murderer stabs him, and pushes him head first into a malmsey-butt to drown in a nightmare of crimson bubbles. (WINE BARREL)

A black flag flies above the palace. Richard has murdered his brother Clarence only just in time; King Edward is dead. All that remains between the hunchback and the crown is the problem of the king's two sons, the little princes. Desperately, the queen sends her own brothers to Ludlow to secure her children's safety, before it is too late. But Richard has a clever friend, his cousin, the Duke of Buckingham who advises they should not be tardy in seizing the heir to the throne.

BUCKINGHAM   My lord, whoever journeys to the prince, for God's sake let not us two stay at home.

RICHARD   My dear cousin, I as a child will go by thy direction. Towards Ludlow then.

The queen's brothers are seized by Richard's men and put to death and Edward, the little Prince of Wales, is brought to London. Hearing this terrible news, the queen decides to go with her younger son, the Duke of York, into sanctuary. Her friend, the Archbishop of York, leads them there.

ELIZABETH   (*clutching her youngest child*) Ay me! I see the ruin of our house: the tiger now hath seiz'd the gentle hind! Come, come, my boy; we will to sanctuary.

At the palace, Richard, Buckingham and others await the arrival of the Prince of Wales. As soon as he arrives, Richard, hopping and capering, like a genial uncle, comes forward to greet him. Buckingham follows Richard.

RICHARD   Welcome, dear cousin, the weary way hath made you melancholy.

EDWARD   No uncle; but our crosses on the way have made it tedious. (*He looks around him.*) I thought my mother and my brother York would long ere this have met us on the way. (*He turns to a nobleman, Lord Hastings.*) Welcome my lord. What, will our mother come?

HASTINGS	(*bowing*) The queen your mother and your brother York have taken sanctuary.
BUCKINGHAM	Fie, what an indirect and peevish course is this of hers! Lord Cardinal, will your grace persuade the queen to send the Duke of York unto his princely brother presently?
ARCHBISHOP	God in Heaven forbid we should infringe the sacred privilege of blessed sanctuary!
BUCKINGHAM	Oft have I heard of sanctuary men, but sanctuary children, never till now.

The cardinal and Hastings leave.

EDWARD	Good lords, make all the speedy haste you may. (*To Richard*) Say, uncle Gloucester, if our brother come, where shall we sojourn till our coronation?
RICHARD	If I may counsel you, some day or two your Highness shall repose you at the Tower.
EDWARD	I do not like the Tower.
BUCKINGHAM	Now in good time here comes the Duke of York.

The young Duke of York, accompanied by Hastings and the cardinal, appears.

EDWARD	Richard of York! how fares our loving brother?

YORK   Well, my lord.

RICHARD   How fares our cousin, noble lord of York?

YORK   I thank you, gentle uncle.

RICHARD   (*to Edward*) My lord, will't please you pass along? Myself will to your mother, to entreat of her to meet you at the Tower.

YORK   (*to his brother*) What, will you go unto the Tower, my lord?

EDWARD   My Lord Protector needs will have it so.

YORK   I shall not sleep in quiet at the Tower.

RICHARD   Why, what should you fear?

YORK   My uncle Clarence' angry ghost: my grandam told me he was murder'd there.

EDWARD   I fear no uncles dead.

RICHARD   Nor none that live, I hope?

The princes leave for the Tower that looms ahead, like a crouching monster. Richard and Buckingham stare after the procession. They see it disappear behind the gates of the fortress, the ravens circling above it. Richard rubs his hands with satisfaction.

With the two little princes, like birds in a cage, locked up in the Tower, Richard's way to the throne is clear. But before he can proclaim himself king, he needs the assent of Lord Hastings, the Lord Chamberlain.

BUCKINGHAM   What shall we do if we perceive Lord Hastings will not yield to our complots?

RICHARD   Chop off his head, man! (*He laughs and lays his arm upon Buckingham's shoulder.*) When I am king, claim thou of me the earldom of Hereford.

BUCKINGHAM   I'll claim that promise at your grace's hand.

In the middle of the night, Sir William Catesby, another friend of Richard's, is sent to rouse Lord Hastings from his bed and sound him out.

HASTINGS   What news, what news in this our tott'ring state?

CATESBY   It is a reeling world indeed, my lord, and will never stand upright till Richard wear the garland of the realm.

HASTINGS   Dost thou mean the crown?

CATESBY   Ay, my good lord.

HASTINGS   I'll have this crown of mine cut from my shoulders before I'll see the crown so foul misplac'd!

CATESBY   God keep your lordship in that gracious mind. (*He hides a grim smile.*)

*Lord Hastings is invited to dinner in the Tower. He supposes it
is to fix the day for the crowning of little Prince Edward as
England's rightful king. Why else should Richard, the Lord
Protector, summon him? Seated at the table, he finds Ely,
Buckingham and other nobles.*

HASTINGS   Now, noble peers, the cause why we are met is to determine of
the coronation. When is the royal day?

ELY   Tomorrow is I judge a happy day.

BUCKINGHAM   Who knows the Lord Protector's mind herein?

ELY   Your grace, we think, should soonest know his mind.

BUCKINGHAM   Lord Hastings, you and he are near in love.

HASTINGS   I thank his grace, I know he loves me well; but for his purpose
in the coronation I have not sounded him. But you, my
honourable lords, may name the time, and in the duke's behalf
I'll give my voice –

ELY   In happy time, here comes the duke himself!

RICHARD   (*entering, all affable*) My noble lords and cousins all, good
morrow!

BUCKINGHAM   Had you not come upon your cue, my lord, William, Lord
Hastings had pronounc'd your part – I mean your voice for
crowning of the king.

RICHARD   Than my Lord Hastings, no man might be bolder! My Lord of Ely, when I was last in Holborn I saw good strawberries in your garden there; I do beseech you, send for some of them!

ELY   Marry, and will, my lord, with all my heart! (*He leaves to send for some.*)

RICHARD   Cousin of Buckingham, a word with you. (*They leave the table together.*)

ELY   (*returning*) Where is the Duke of Gloucester? I have sent for these strawberries.

HASTINGS   His grace looks cheerfully and smooth this morning; there's some conceit or other likes him well. I think there's never a man in Christendom can lesser hide his love or hate than he, for by his face straight shall you know his heart.

Richard returns with Buckingham. Buckingham is looking troubled, Richard savage.

RICHARD   I pray you all, tell me what they deserve that do conspire my death with devilish plots of damned witchcraft, and that have prevail'd upon my body with their hellish charms?

HASTINGS   I say, my lord, they have deserved death.

RICHARD   Then be your eyes the witness of their evil! (*Drags up a sleeve to show his withered arm.*) See how I am bewitch'd! And this is Edward's wife, that monstrous witch, consorted with that harlot, strumpet Shore, that by their witchcraft thus have marked me!

HASTINGS   If they have done this deed, my noble lord –

RICHARD   If? Thou protector of this damned strumpet, talk'st thou to me
            of ifs? Thou art a traitor: off with his head! Now by Saint Paul
            I will not dine until I see the same.

*Richard storms out, and is followed by the others, leaving the
dismayed Hastings. Two sinister figures of the guard appear
behind him. One of them puts his hand on Hasting's shoulder
and squeezes it. Hastings lowers his head realizing that he is
doomed. He is led away.*

A servant enters the room bearing a dish of strawberries that he places on the table. The other nobles return with Richard and Buckingham. They seat themselves and dishes are brought in. A covered plate is set before Richard. He lifts the lid. Hastings' severed head glares out. Silence falls upon the table.

RICHARD   (*sighing*) So dear I lov'd the man that I must weep. (*He bows his head.*)

BUCKINGHAM   (*jumping up*) Long live King Richard, England's worthy king!

LORDS   Long live King Richard!

At last the hunchback, having climbed a ladder of murders, is king. But while he walks in glory, three women stand in wretchedness and grief before the Tower. Richard's unhappy wife, the Lady Anne; the queen, mother of the two little princes; and the mother of the hunchback himself, the Duchess of York.

DUCHESS   O my accursed womb, the bed of death! A cockatrice hast thou
            hatch'd to the world, whose unavoided eye is murderous!

ANNE   He hates me . . . and will, no doubt, shortly be rid of me.

QUEEN   Pity, you ancient stones, those tender babes. Rough cradle for
            such little pretty ones! Use my babies well.

*In the great hall of the palace, thronged with nobles, King
Richard, crowned and robed, hops between the bowing figures. His cloak is huge and scarlet and flows after him like a
river of blood. He ascends the throne and beckons to Buckingham who comes to kneel beside him.*

RICHARD   Shall we wear these glories for a day? Or shall they last?

BUCKINGHAM   For ever let them last!

RICHARD   (*shaking his head*) Young Edward lives – think now what I would speak.

BUCKINGHAM   Say on, my loving lord.

RICHARD   Cousin, thou wast not wont to be so dull. Shall I be plain? I wish the bastards dead. What say'st thou now?

BUCKINGHAM   Your grace may do your pleasure.

RICHARD   Tut, tut, thou art all ice. Say, have I thy consent that they shall die?

BUCKINGHAM   Give me some little breath, some pause, before I positively speak in this.

Bowing, Buckingham withdraws. Richard stares after him, malevolently.

RICHARD   High-reaching Buckingham grows circumspect. (*He beckons to a page, who approaches. Richard murmurs in his ear.*) Know'st thou not any whom corrupting gold will tempt unto a close exploit of death? (*The page nods and hastens away. Richard glares about him. He sees Buckingham smiling. He smiles in return.*) No more shall he be neighbour to my counsels. Come hither, Catesby! Rumour it abroad that Anne, my wife, is very grievous sick. (*Catesby looks startled.*) I say again, give out that Anne, my queen, is sick and like to die. About it! (*Catesby departs.*)

In his bedchamber, Richard frowns into the mirror. To keep the crown he's seized, he needs a better marriage. Once rid of Anne, he will marry Elizabeth, sister of the two little princes who still languish in the Tower.

The page enters, accompanied by a desperate, needy-looking gentleman by the name of Sir James Tyrrel. Richard gestures for the page to leave.

RICHARD	Dar'st thou resolve to kill a friend of mine?
TYRREL	Please you, but I had rather kill two enemies.
RICHARD	Why then thou hast it; two deep enemies. Tyrrel, I mean those bastards in the Tower.
TYRREL	I will dispatch it straight! (*He hastens away. No sooner has he left than Buckingham enters.*)
BUCKINGHAM	My lord, I have consider'd in my mind the late request that you did sound me in.
RICHARD	(*with an airy wave of his hand*) Well, let that rest.
BUCKINGHAM	My lord, I claim the gift, my due by promise, th' earldom of Hereford —
RICHARD	(*as if not hearing*) I do remember me, Henry the Sixth did prophesy that Richmond should be king, when Richmond was a little peevish boy.
BUCKINGHAM	My lord, your promise for the earldom!
RICHARD	I am not in the giving vein today. Thou troublest me; I am not in the vein. (*Richard moves away, leaving Buckingham red-faced and alone.*)

BUCKINGHAM   And is it thus? Repays he my deep service with such contempt?
Made I him king for this? O, let me think on Hastings, and be
gone!

*If Buckingham had proved a broken reed, Tyrrel was made of
sterner stuff. With the help of two sturdy assistants, he
smothers the two children while they sleep.*

*In the royal apartments, Richard, surrounded by servants,
attires himself splendidly in front of a mirror.*

RICHARD   The sons of Edward sleep in Abraham's bosom, and Anne my wife hath bid this world good night. Now, for I know that Richmond aims at young Elizabeth, my brother's daughter, and by that knot looks proudly on the crown – to her go I, a jolly thriving wooer. (*Richard hops but suddenly Catesby stands in his path.*)

RICHARD   (*with irritation*) Good or bad news, that thou com'st in so bluntly?

CATESBY   Bad news, my lord: Ely is fled to Richmond, and Buckingham, back'd with the hardy Welshmen, is in the field, and still his power increaseth.

RICHARD   (*clenching his fists*) Go, muster men. We must be brief, when traitors brave the field.

But the news goes from bad to worse.

MESSENGER   My lord, the army of great Buckingham is –

RICHARD   Out on you, owls! Nothing but songs of death? (*He strikes him. The messenger falls down.*) There, take thou that, till thou bring better news!

MESSENGER   (*getting up*) The news I have to tell your majesty is that by sudden flood and fall of water Buckingham's army is dispers'd and scatter'd, and he himself wander'd away alone.

RICHARD   I cry thee mercy; there is my purse to cure that blow of thine. (*He flings some money at him.*)

44

Richard goes to the entrance of his tent and speaks to his officers.

RICHARD   Stir with the lark tomorrow, gentle Norfolk.

NORFOLK   I warrant you, my lord.

RICHARD   (*to another officer*) Give me a bowl of wine. I have not that alacrity of spirit nor cheer of mind that I was wont to have. Leave me.

Richard is alone in his tent. He sits wearily down on his bed and drinks a glass of wine in one gulp. He puts the glass on the table and watches the light of the lamp. He sleeps. The lamp begins to burn blue. Strange, flimsy white wisps enter the tent. They gather round the sleeping king. Little by little, they assume more definite shapes. They are the ghosts of his victims. They go in circles above Richard, one by one coming closer to him. Richards stirs and tosses in his sleep.

GHOST OF CLARENCE   Poor Clarence, by thy guile betray'd to death – tomorrow in the battle think on me.

ALL GHOSTS   Despair and die!

GHOST OF HASTINGS   In a bloody battle end thy days! Think on Lord Hastings!

ALL GHOSTS   Despair and die!

GHOSTS OF TWO LITTLE PRINCES	Dream on thy cousins smother'd in the Tower.
ALL GHOSTS	Despair and die!
GHOST OF ANNE	Richard, thy wife, that wretched Anne, thy wife. Tomorrow in the battle think on me.
ALL GHOSTS	Despair and die!
GHOST OF BUCKINGHAM	The first was I that help'd thee to the crown; the last was I that felt thy tyranny. O, in the battle think of Buckingham, and die in terror of thy guiltiness.

Richard awakes and looks around him in terror.

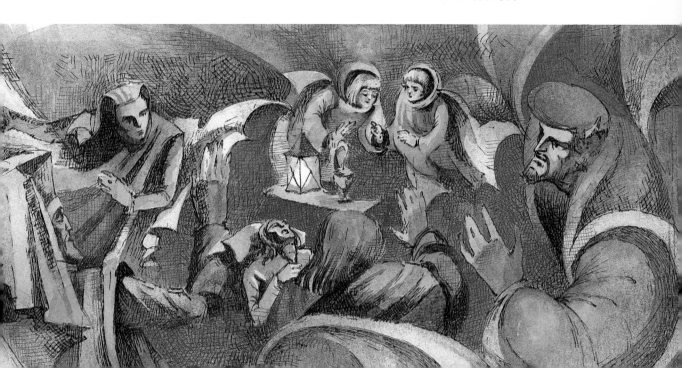

RICHARD   Soft, I did but dream. What do I fear? Myself? (*He sees his huge shadow on the wall of the tent and smiles at it.*) Richard loves Richard: that is, I and I. Is there a murderer here? (*He draws his dagger.*) No. Yes, I am. Then fly. What, from myself?

Richard pours wine into a goblet. His hands are shaking. He spills some wine, which spreads like a pool of blood over the table. He drinks the wine in one gulp.

RICHARD   Let not our babbling dreams affright our souls; conscience is but a word that cowards use, devis'd at first to keep the strong in awe. Our strong arms be our conscience, swords our law.

Richard is himself again.

On the hillside, in the early morning mist, Richard, on his great white horse, rides up and down before his troops. He looks up to the sky.

RICHARD   The sun will not be seen today. Not shine today? Why, what is that to me more than to Richmond?

He looks towards the place where Richmond's troops are waiting. Suddenly a sun-ray cuts through the clouds. Richmond's armour flares up in gold. He is ahead of his troops.

NORFOLK   (*riding up to Richard*) Arm, arm, my lord; the foe vaunts in the field!

RICHARD   Come, bustle, bustle! (*He addresses his troops.*) March on! Join bravely. Let us to it pell-mell, if not to Heaven, then hand in hand to hell! Fight, gentlemen of England! Fight, bold yeomen! Draw, archers, draw your arrows to the head. Advance, our standards. Set upon our foes!

He waves, and the advance begins, down the hillside towards the enemy. Richard's troops mingle with Richmond's troops in battle, Richard laying about him like a madman. At last, his horse is killed. He scrambles to his feet and fights on.

RICHARD   A horse! A horse! My kingdom for a horse!

Catesby rides by.

CATESBY   Withdraw, my lord. I'll help you to a horse.

RICHARD   Slave, I have set my life upon a cast, and I will stand the hazard of the die! I think there be six Richmonds in the field: five have I slain today instead of him!

He stumbles away, killing and killing. Suddenly he confronts the tall, golden figure of Richmond. He raises his sword. The air is full of whispers. He strikes out, but his sword is heavy. Richmond in a single blow cuts off Richard's head.

The crown is brought to Richmond. He puts it on and all kneel before him.

RICHMOND   (*staring around the battlefield that is littered with the dead*) England hath long been mad and scarr'd herself: the brother blindly shed the brother's blood; the father rashly slaughter'd his own son; the son, compell'd, been butcher to the sire. All this divided York and Lancaster – O, now let Richmond and Elizabeth, the true succeeders of each royal house, by God's fair ordinance conjoin together! Now civil wounds are stopp'd, peace lives again. That she may long live here, God say amen!

The curtain falls.